Science Experiments

WITH

COLOR

Sally Nankivell-Aston
and Dorothy Jackson

W
FRANKLIN WATTS
A Division of Grolier Publishing

NEW YORK • LONDON • HONG KONG • SYDNEY
DANBURY, CONNECTICUT

Acknowledgements: Cover: Steve Shott; AKG London p.6br (Musée Condé, Chantilly); Bruce Coleman pp.4b (Christer Fredriksson), 5bl (Jules Cowan), 14t (Joe McDonald); Image Bank pp.9bl (Jeff Spielman), 9br (Andy Caulfield); Oxford Scientific Films pp.4m (Alistair Shay), 5tr, 5br (Robin Redfern), 12b (Zig Leszczynski), 29tr (Michael Fogden), 29b (Wendy Shattil and Bob Rozinski); Panos Pictures pp.17m (Ray Wood), 25tr (James Bedding); Science Photo Library pp. 4t (John Mead), 10b (Vaughan Fleming), 19t (Jerry Mason), 27t (Jon Wilson). Thanks, too, to our models: Erin Bhogal, Perry Christian, Bonita Crawley, Jaimé Leigh Pyle, Jordan Oldfield, Nicholas Payne, Jennifer Quaife, and Alexander Smale

Series editor: Rachel Cooke; Designer: Mo Choy
Picture research: Susan Mennell; Photography: Ray Moller, unless otherwise acknowledged

First published in 2000 by Franklin Watts

First American edition 2000 by Franklin Watts
A Division of Grolier Publishing
90 Sherman Turnpike, Danbury, CT 06816

Visit Franklin Watts on the Internet at:
http://publishing.grolier.com

Library of Congress Cataloging-in-Publication Data

Nankivell-Aston, Sally.
    Science experiments with color / Sally Nankivell-Aston and Dorothy Jackson.
        p.cm.
    Includes index.
    Summary: Explores the properties of color through experiments using materials that are readily available in both homes and schools.
    ISBN 0-531-14581-6 (library ed.) 0-531-15442-4 (pbk.)
    1. Color--Juvenile literature. 2. Color--Experiments-- Juvenile literature. [1.Color--Experiments. 2. Experiments.]
    I. Jackson, Dorothy. II. Title.

QC495.5. N36 2000
535.6'078--dc21
                                        99-088992

Contents

Color All Around

L OOK AROUND YOU WHEREVER you are, and you see colors. Colors can be bright or dull, "warm" or "cold," can blend together or contrast, be natural or artificial. Look at the pictures and see how many shades of the same color you can spot.

What is your favorite color? Is it the same color that your friend likes best? Discover all about your favorite colors as you do the experiments in this book.

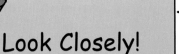

Be Amazed!

By doing the experiments in this book, you can find out some amazing things about color. You will find out about the colors of paint and light, how we see colors, and how colors can be useful to us, other animals, and plants. Some experiments may answer questions that you already ask about color. Some may make you think of more!

Look Closely!

Scientists always ask lots of questions and observe carefully. When you are doing experiments in this book, look closely to see what is happening, and keep accurate records of your results. Don't be upset if your predictions do not always turn out to be correct, as scientists (and that includes you) learn a lot from unexpected results.

Be Careful!

Always make sure an adult knows that you are doing an experiment. Ask for help if you need to use sharp tools, heat things, or use chemicals. Follow the step-by-step instructions carefully, and remember — be a safe scientist!

Mixing Paints

Have you ever noticed how many different colors of paint you can buy? Each paint contains a natural or artificial pigment to give it color. All these color pigments are actually made from mixing only three colors: red, yellow, and blue. These are the primary colors of pigments. Find out more in this first experiment.

✓ You Will Need:
- ✓ red, yellow, and blue poster paints
- ✓ large pieces of white paper
- ✓ 3 paintbrushes
- ✓ drinking straw
- ✓ 3 saucers

1 Put a small pool of paint on each saucer — one color onto each. The paint must be runny, so add water if necessary and mix in with a paintbrush. Use a separate paintbrush for each color.

2 Use the paintbrushes to scatter drops of the three colors, each color on a separate piece of paper. Then put drops of a second color as shown. Don't let the drops touch each other!

In Action

Today, most paint pigments are made from artificial ingredients. However, they used to be made from natural materials like plants, rocks, and dead insects. The pigment for the blue paint in this 15th-century picture was made by crushing the semiprecious stone, lapis lazuli.

3 Use the straw to blow the paint across the paper so that the colors mix.

4 What happens when red and yellow mix? What happens when red and blue mix? What happens when yellow and blue mix? The mixed colors are called secondary colors. Put your answers on a table like the one below.

Keep Thinking

How would you make a paint lighter? How could you make paint darker? How could you get different shades of green?

PRIMARY COLORS MIXED	SECONDARY COLOR MADE
red and yellow	
yellow and blue	
red and blue	

5 Now find out what color you get if all three primary colors are mixed together. This is called a tertiary color.

Don't Stop There

● Drop oil-based inks (marbling inks) onto water in a tray. Swirl the colors around with a toothpick. What colors do you get? "Capture" the colors by gently lowering a piece of paper on top of the water and then removing it carefully.

● Go to a craft store and get some paint charts. How many different types of blue are there? How many different types of red are there?

Mixing Light

ALTHOUGH LIGHT USUALLY looks white, it is really made up of different colors. The primary colors of light are red, green, and blue. They are not exactly the same as those in pigments, and they don't mix in the same way. Find out how these colors of light mix in this experiment.

1 Fix a color filter over the end of each cardboard tube with tape.

2 Hold a tube and shine a flashlight beam down the open end onto a pale-colored wall in a dark room. Ask your friends to do the same with the other two tubes. Can you see each color on the wall?

Keep Thinking

Look back at pages 6 and 7 to find out which of the primary colors of light are the same as the primary colors of pigments.

3 What color do you predict you will see when the red and green lights are mixed together? Find out by making the two colors of light overlap on the wall.

4 In the same way, find out what happens when red and blue lights mix, then green and blue. The resulting colors are called the secondary colors of light.

PRIMARY COLORS MIXED	SECONDARY COLOR MADE
red and green	
red and blue	
green and blue	

5 Record your results on a table like this one.

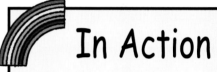

In Action

Dramatic lighting effects are achieved by mixing different colored spotlights in theaters, at rock concerts, or even on a dance floor.

Don't Stop There

● Find out what color you get when all three are mixed together.

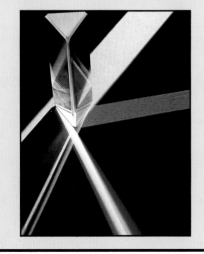

● You can split white light into its different colors using a prism. Shine a strong flashlight beam through a prism placed on a light piece of paper. What colors can you see on the paper?

Seeing Colors

IMAGINE WHAT THE world would look like if you couldn't see any colors! We have special cells called cones in our eyes that let us see in color. There are about 7 million cones in each of your eyes!

iris

retina

pupil

lens

cone

This diagram shows the different parts of the eye and a close-up of some of its cones, which are found in the retina. Some cones see red, some blue, and others green. Find out more in this eye-opening experiment!

✓ You Will Need:

- ✓ colored paper (red, green, and blue)
- ✓ 4 pieces of white 8 1/2 x 11 cardboard
- ✓ scissors
- ✓ pencil
- ✓ ruler
- ✓ glue

❶ Cut out red, green, and blue squares, each measuring 4 x 4 in (10 x 10 cm).

❷ Stick each one onto a separate piece of white cardboard.

In Action

This is a TV screen close-up! Pictures on the screen are made up of tiny dots or stripes of green, red, and blue — the primary colors of light. Looked at from a distance, these colors mix and merge to form the multicolored picture we see.

3 Now stare hard at the cardboard with the red square for 30 seconds.

4 Then quickly look at a plain white piece of cardboard. What do you see?

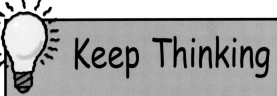

5 Now repeat the experiment in the same way first with the green square, then with the blue.

6 What shape do you see on the white piece of cardboard, each time? What color is it? Add your results to a table like the one below.

COLOR OF SQUARE	red	green	blue
SHAPE SEEN ON WHITE CARDBOARD			
COLOR SEEN ON WHITE CARDBOARD			

Keep Thinking

As you stared at a colored square, the cones that see that color got tired, so only the cones that see the other two colors were working. How does this explain what you saw when you looked at the plain white cardboard?

Don't Stop There

● Repeat the experiment with a yellow square. What color is the image this time?

● People who are color blind cannot see certain colors. Look at this picture. Can you see the number? Some color-blind people would not be able to read the number picked out in shades of green.

Standing Out

COLORS ARE OFTEN USED to make things stand out and be noticed. For example, cyclists often wear bright colors so motorists can see them easily. Find out which colors stand out best in this experiment.

✔️ **You Will Need:**
- ✔️ 6 thick marker pens, various colors
- ✔️ 6 pieces of white cardboard
- ✔️ tape measure
- ✔️ a friend

1 Draw a large exclamation point on each piece of white cardboard using a different colored marker pen each time. Make sure they are all about the same size and shape to make the test fair.

2 Predict which color can be seen from the farthest distance.

Keep Thinking

Male birds are often brightly colored so they can be seen easily. Why do you think they want to be noticed?

In Action

Some animals are brightly colored to warn other animals that they are dangerous or taste disgusting. This tree frog is poisonous. Its color warns other animals not to eat it.

3 Ask a friend to stand in a playground or garden. Stand a long way away from your friend, and hold up one of the pieces of cardboard.

4 Gradually walk closer to your friend and ask him or her to say when the exclamation point can be seen clearly. Measure the distance to your friend.

5 Repeat the test with the other colors and record your results in a table like this:

COLOR OF EXCLAMATION POINT	DISTANCE IT CAN BE SEEN FROM

6 Which color was easiest to see? Which was most difficult? Which color would be best to use to write DANGER on a warning sign?

Don't Stop There

● Cut out some exclamation points from white paper, all the same size and shape. Stick each one on a different colored piece of cardboard or paper. Repeat the experiment to see which colored background makes the white exclamation point stand out most.

● Look around at signs on the roads and streets. Which colors have been used to make the signs?

Now You See Me, Now You Don't!

ALTHOUGH SOME ANIMALS are brightly colored to be noticed, others have dull colors to help them hide. They are camouflaged among the colors of their natural environment. This means that predators can hunt without being seen, and prey animals are less likely to be caught. Find out more about camouflage in this experiment.

In Action

Chameleons are camouflage experts! As the colors around them change, their skin color changes to match.

✓ You Will Need:

- ✓ brown and black felt-tip pens
- ✓ 2 hard-boiled eggs (brown)
- ✓ a range of natural materials collected from a park or garden
- ✓ different art materials in assorted colors

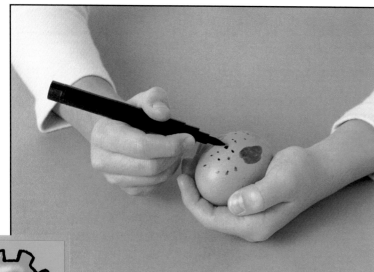

1 First add speckles to your eggs with the felt-tip pens to make them look like this quail egg.

2 Now make two nests, one using the art materials and the other using the natural materials you have collected. Use lots of bright colors for the nest made of art materials but make the natural nest with roughly the same colors as on the egg.

3 Place an egg in each nest and look at the nests from a short distance.

Keep Thinking

Patterns help camouflage an animal because they break up the outline of the animal's body. Zebras live on wide grassy plains, tigers in shady jungles. What other animals have patterns to help them hide?

4 Which egg is easier to see? Why is it easy to see? Which is more difficult? Why? Which nest hides the egg better? Why do you think eggs need to be well hidden?

Don't Stop There

● Put the nests in a backyard or park. How long does it take your friends to spot each one? Which is easiest to find? Why?

● Make flowers out of different colors of tissue paper. Scatter them around the backyard. Which colors are easier to see and which are more difficult?

Hot or Cold?

WHY DO PEOPLE OFTEN WEAR white clothes on hot summer days and black clothes during cold winter months? Do you think white clothes make you feel cooler and black clothes make you feel warmer? Find out in this experiment.

✓ You Will Need:
- ✓ a small piece of black fur fabric
- ✓ a small piece of white fur fabric
- ✓ 2 thermometers
- ✓ tape

1 Look at the thermometers and make a record of the temperature readings before you start the experiment. They should be the same on both.

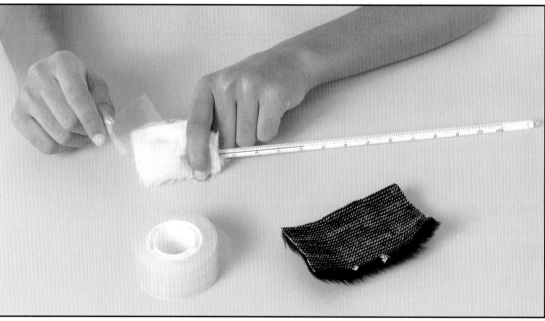

2 Wrap a small piece of white fur fabric around one of the thermometer bulbs and a black piece around the other. The pieces should be the same size and big enough to wrap around the bulb once. Hold the fabric in place with a small piece of tape.

Keep Thinking

What color clothes do you think would make you feel cool on a hot day?

3 Set both thermometers on a sunny windowsill, with the tape underneath. Read the temperatures of each thermometer every 15 minutes for 2 hours. Make a table like this to record your results.

TIME	TEMPERATURE OF WHITE THERMOMETER	TEMPERATURE OF BLACK THERMOMETER
0 mins		
15 mins		
30 mins		
45 mins		
1 hr		
1 hr 15 mins		
1 hr 30 mins		
1 hr 45 mins		
2 hrs		

4 Which thermometer became hotter? Did the white fabric or the black fabric let the most heat through? Some colors reflect more heat than others, while others absorb heat better. Which fabric reflected more heat? Do you think white fabrics would keep you cooler on a hot day? Would black fabrics make you feel warmer?

In Action

People who live in hot countries often wear light-colored, loose-fitting clothes to help them keep cool. This man lives in the hot desert regions of Mali in West Africa.

Don't Stop There

● Repeat the experiment using different colors of fur fabric or felt. Find out which colors absorb the most heat.

● Put a large piece of fur fabric with a black-and-white design (e.g. imitation cow's skin) in strong sunlight for about half an hour. Stroke your hand over the fabric. Can you feel a difference in temperature between the black and white areas?

A Color Detective

A DETECTIVE FOUND A MYSTERIOUS, unsigned note from a criminal. She knew it had been written using one of two black marker pens: One pen belonged to suspect A, and one pen belonged to suspect B. The pens were different brands, and the detective knew how to find out quickly which suspect had written the note. She used a scientific process called chromatography, which separates colors. Here is how the detective solved the case.

You Will Need:
- 2 black water-soluble marker pens of different brands
- 2 coffee filters
- 2 drinking glasses
- eyedropper
- water in a jar

1 In the center of each coffee filter, make a small spot about 1/2 in (1 cm) in diameter using one marker pen for each filter. Place a filter on top of each glass.

2 Use the eyedropper to drop water carefully onto each colored ink spot. Put the same number of drops on each one to make the test fair.

3 Look closely to see what happens to the color spot from each pen as the ink dissolves in the water and spreads out.

In Action

Chromatography helps scientists study diseases, such as cancer. They use it to test tiny samples taken from the human body. There are small differences in the pattern made from a healthy sample and the one made from a sample with the disease.

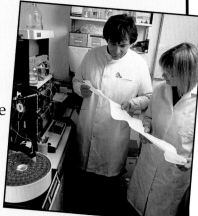

Keep Thinking

Look back at pages 6 and 7 to find out what colors are made when different colored paints or pigments are mixed. Did this experiment show the results you expected?

4 Do both ink spots make the same pattern? What colors make up the black color of each marker? Were you surprised?

5 How could the detective use the results from this experiment to find out who had written the note?

Don't Stop There

● Try repeating the experiment using markers of different colors and find out what colors each one is made from.

● Use chromatography to find out if black writing ink used in fountain pens is made of a mixture of colors. If so, are they the same colors as those in black marker pen ink?

Appearing Pictures

Some CHEMICALS CHANGE from transparent to a color in heat. Amaze your friends with this experiment and make a picture appear magically on plain white paper.

Safety: Ask an adult to help you iron the paper in step 3.

1 Use the paintbrush to draw a picture with lemon juice on the paper.

2 Leave the paper to dry so you can hardly see the picture. You have hidden your picture! Show the paper to a friend and ask him or her what they can see on the paper.

Keep Thinking

What materials can you think of that change color when they are heated or burned?

3 Ask an adult to iron over the back of the paper (that is, the side you did not draw on) with a hot iron.

In Action

Prisoners used to use saliva or sweat to write secret messages, which could be smuggled out to their friends. The messages could only be seen and read when they were heated.

4 Show your friend the paper now. What can be seen? What has changed in the heat to make your picture appear?

Don't Stop There

● Do you think other transparent liquids change in the same way when they are heated? Try the experiment using lemonade, then vinegar. What other liquids could you try?

● Ask an adult to light a match. Blow the flame out and look closely at the color of the wood. How has heat affected the color of the wood? In what other ways has the wood changed?

Color Tests

YOU CAN USE COLOR to find out more about the foods we eat and the chemicals we use at home. Some things are acid; some are the opposite, alkaline; and some are neutral, which is in between. Find out more in this experiment.

Safety: Ask an adult for help with step 1.

1 Chop up some red cabbage leaves and put them into a saucepan with a little water. Heat the pan and boil the cabbage for a few minutes.

2 Let it cool and strain the juice into the bowl. Throw away the cabbage but keep the juice. The juice is for testing the chemicals to find out if they are acid or alkaline. We call it an indicator. What color is your indicator? It may vary, depending on the type of saucepan you use.

In Action

This is litmus paper, which scientists use to test for acid and alkaline. Sometimes they test for acid rain, which damages plant life, buildings, and stone statues.

3 Now add four drops of cabbage water to each saucer containing the kitchen chemicals.

Look closely to see the color changes of each liquid. Record your results in a table like the one shown.

	COLOR WHEN CABBAGE WATER IS ADDED	IS IT ACID, ALKALINE, OR NEUTRAL?
bicarbonate of soda		
lemon juice		
dishwashing liquid		
salt		

4 Red cabbage water is a natural indicator that can be used to tell if substances are acid or alkaline. It turns red in acids and blue-green in alkaline substances. In neutral substances that are neither acid nor alkaline, its color does not change. Can you tell which of your chemicals are acid, alkaline, or neutral? Add this to your table.

Don't Stop There

● Repeat the experiment to test other foods and common chemicals. You could try milk, orange juice, and sugar. BE CAREFUL! Ask an adult first in case you want to test something that is harmful. DO NOT use strong or bleach-based cleaning solutions. Record your results in a table.

● Try the experiment again with the water from boiling fresh beets (they need longer cooking than cabbage). What color changes do you get this time? Are they the same as the colors made with red cabbage water?

Dyeing for Color

WHAT COLOR IS YOUR favorite shirt or sweater? It was probably dyed using artificial chemicals, but how do you think the first dyes were made? Find out how to dye your own fabric using natural colors from everyday things in this experiment.

Safety: Ask an adult for help with this experiment.

1 First predict what color dye each of the different foods will make. Record your ideas in a table like the one shown.

2 Prepare the fabrics to be dyed by tying elastic bands tightly at intervals along each piece as shown in the picture.

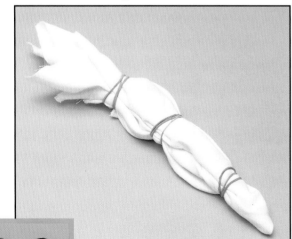

You Will Need:
- ✔ 4 pieces of white cotton fabric, such as handkerchiefs or pieces of an old tee-shirt
- ✔ onion skins from at least 2 onions
- ✔ a fresh beet chopped into small pieces
- ✔ red cabbage chopped up   ✔ spoon
- ✔ 3 tea bags
- ✔ 4 small bowls
- ✔ elastic bands
- ✔ saucepan
- ✔ sieve

FOOD USED	PREDICTED COLOR	ACTUAL COLOR
onion skins		
beet		
red cabbage		
tea bag		

3 Now make your first dye with the onion skins. Put them into the saucepan and pour on enough water to cover them.

Ask an adult to boil the skins until you can see that the color from the skins has gone into the water.

24

4 Use the sieve to strain the colored liquid into a bowl. This is your dye. Put a piece of fabric into the hot liquid and stir it around with a spoon.

5 Make dyes with the other foods in the same way, and put one piece of fabric into each bowl. Leave it overnight, then take out the fabrics and remove the elastic bands.

Keep Thinking

Some people make pictures by painting wax onto fabric then dyeing it. Then they iron the fabric between paper to remove the wax. This kind of dyeing is called batik. What effect do you think the wax has?

6 Look closely to see what has happened to the fabric. What color has the dye from each food turned the fabric? Were your predictions correct? What has happened where the elastic was tied around the fabric? Why?

Don't Stop There

● Try to make dye from other foods and plants. You could try petals from brightly colored flowers, grass, blackberries, and coffee. Predict the color first, then make the dyes to find the results.

● Repeat the experiment using different fabrics, such as wool or synthetics, to find out if all cloth absorbs colors from plants in the same way.

Going Green!

WHAT COLOR ARE THE LEAVES of most plants? Do you know why? Plants make their food (a sugar called glucose) using the energy from sunlight, water, carbon dioxide, and a green-colored chemical called chlorophyll. This process is called photosynthesis. Chlorophyll is found mostly in the leaves. Do this experiment and find out more about going green.

✓ You Will Need:
- ✓ two similar green-leafed house-plants (Don't use a plant with variegated leaves)
- ✓ a dark cupboard
- ✓ labels
- ✓ pen

1 Label the plants A and B. Look closely at the color of the leaves. Make sure that the plants are well watered.

2 Put plant A into a very dark cupboard — make sure no light can reach it. Put plant B in a light place. Leave both plants for about a week.

In Action

Leaves of plants are not always the same shade of green because they contain other pigments as well as chlorophyll. This copper beech still makes its food by photosynthesis, but the green chlorophyll is masked by the copper pigments.

3 Take plant A out of the cupboard and place it next to plant B. What do you notice about each plant? Do they still look the same?

4 If the plant has no energy from light, it cannot make food and the leaves lose their green color. What do you think will happen if you put plant B into the cupboard and leave plant A in the light? Test to find out.

5 Compare the plants after one week. What do you notice now? What do you think was the reason for the changes in the plants?

Keep Thinking

In autumn, the leaves on many trees change color when they die and fall off the tree. Why do you think the leaves lose their green color?

Don't Stop There

Get a plant that has red or patterned leaves. What do you think will happen this time if you repeat the experiment? Test to find out.

Fabulous Flowers

WHAT IS YOUR FAVORITE color? Do you think insects have favorite colors, too? Find out about why flowers have such fabulous colors in this experiment.

Note: It is better to do this experiment in spring or summer, when there are plenty of insects around.

✔️ **You Will Need:**
- ✔️ red, blue, green, yellow, purple, and orange paint
- ✔️ 7 white paper plates
- ✔️ scissors
- ✔️ honey

1 First turn the paper plates into "flowers." Cut petal shapes around the edge as shown and paint each plate a different color. Leave one white.

2 Put a teaspoon of honey in the center of each plate. Place the plates in open spaces around a garden or playground on a sunny day.

Keep Thinking Look back at pages 12 and 13 to find out which color was easiest to see when you made your signs. Is this the same color as the flower that attracted the most insects in this experiment?

3 Watch carefully for half an hour to see how many insects and other small creatures visit each flower.

Keep a record in a table like the one shown.

FLOWER COLOR	NUMBER OF INSECTS VISITING
white	
red	
blue	
yellow	
green	
purple	
orange	

In Action

Like many insects, this hummingbird is attracted to brightly colored flowers and feeds from the sugary nectar inside them. Some pollen from the flowers sticks to the hummingbird and is taken to the next flower it visits. This flower is now able to form seeds, so new plants can grow. This process is called pollination.

4 Which color flower do the insects visit most? Have you seen lots of real flowers of this color? Why is it useful to flowers if insects visit them? Which color do insects visit least? Do you see many flowers of this color? If not, why not?

Don't Stop There

● In an area of wildflowers, find out the most common flower color. Is it the same color that you found insects visited most?

● Repeat the experiment, but this time keep a record of the type of insects that visit the flowers as well. Do different types of insects prefer different colors?

Glossary

This glossary gives the meaning of each word as it is used in this book.

Acid A chemical that is acid turns indicators red.

Acid rain Acidic pollution from factories and car exhausts carried in the air can dissolve in the water held in clouds. This water then falls as acid rain.

Alkaline A chemical that is alkaline turns indicators blue/green.

Batik A method of producing patterned fabrics using wax to stop dye(s) from coloring parts of the fabric.

Camouflage Colorings or patterns to make an animal, person, or vehicle difficult to see in its surroundings.

Carbon dioxide A gas in the air that plants use to make food in the process of photosynthesis.

Cell Very small parts of all living things. Cells are sometimes called the building blocks of life.

Chlorophyll The green chemical in plants that enables them to make food using energy from sunlight, carbon dioxide from the air, and water from the ground in a process called photosynthesis.

Chromatography A technique used to separate a mixture of different chemicals, such as pigments, into its different parts.

Color blind People who are color blind are unable to see certain colors.

Color filter A transparent piece of colored material that allows only light of that color to pass through it.

Cones Cells in the retina of the eye that enable us to see things in color.

Diameter The straight line from one edge of a circle to the other passing through its center.

Dye To dye something is to change its color by soaking it in a specially colored liquid. The liquid is also called a dye.

Energy People, plants, and animals need energy to live. Machines need energy to work. Energy comes from lots of different sources. Burning gasoline gives a car its energy. Food gives us our energy.

Experiment A fair test done to find out more about something or to answer a question. Sometimes called an investigation.

Fair test A scientific test to find an accurate result. To keep the test fair, when you are experimenting, only one part (variable) must be changed and all the other parts (variables) must stay the same.

Filter paper Absorbent paper with very fine holes in it.

Glucose A type of sugar.

Indicator A substance used to find out, or indicate, if a chemical is acid or alkaline.

Iris The colored part of the eye that surrounds the pupil.

Lapis lazuli A semiprecious blue mineral that used to be used to make a bright blue pigment for paints. Today, lapis lazuli is more often used in jewelry.

Lens In an eye, the lens focuses the light that enters through the pupil to form a clear image on the retina.

Litmus paper Paper that contains an indicator so that it changes color when dipped in something that is acid or alkaline.

Nectar A sweet liquid made in the flowers of some plants to attract insects and other animals to visit them to help the process of pollination.

Neutral A chemical that is neutral is neither acid nor alkaline. Pure water is neutral.

Photosynthesis The process by which plants use energy from the sun and chlorophyll to make their food.

Pigment A material used to color paints, inks, and dyes.

Pollen Very small grains from the male part of a flower.

Pollination The process by which pollen is transferred from the male part of a flower to a female part to make seeds from which new plants can grow.

Predators Animals that hunt and eat other animals for food.

Predict To guess what will happen in an experiment before doing it.

Prey Animals that are hunted and eaten by other animals for food.

Primary colors of light The three colors of light — red, green, and blue — which can be mixed together to create all other light colors.

Primary colors of pigment The three pigment colors — red, blue, and yellow — which can be mixed together to create all other colors.

Prism A solid piece of transparent glass or plastic (often looking like a pyramid) that can be used to split white light into its colors.

Pupil A small hole in the iris that lets light into the eye.

Quail A small short-tailed bird that is a member of the partridge family.

Result(s) The outcome of an experiment.

Retina The back of the inside of the eye made up of light-sensitive cells.

Saliva The liquid in your mouth that helps you digest and swallow your food.

Secondary color The color made when two primary colors mix.

Temperature How hot or cold something is. Temperature is measured in degrees Celsius or Fahrenheit.

Tertiary color The color made when three primary colors mix.

Thermometer An instrument to measure temperature.

Transparent Completely see-through.

Index